Heads or Tails?

Exploring Probability Through Games

Greg Roza

PowerMath™

The Rosen Publishing Group's
PowerKids Press™
New York

Published in 2004 by The Rosen Publishing Group, Inc.
29 East 21st Street, New York, NY 10010

Book Design: Ron A. Churley
Photo Credits: Cover, p. 11 © SuperStock; cover (inset), p. 16 (inset) © PhotoDisc; pp. 4–5 © Richard
During/Stone; p. 5 (top inset) © Ken Chernus/Taxi; p. 5 (bottom inset) © Lisa Podgur Cuscuna/Index Stock;
p. 7 © Jose Luis Pelaez, Inc./Corbis; pp. 8–9 © Reuters NewMedia Inc./Corbis; p. 8 (inset) © Howard
Sokol/Index Stock; p. 10 (inset), 18 (inset) by Ron A. Churley; pp. 13, 14, 15, 18–19 by Michael Tsanis;
pp. 16–17 © SW Productions/Index Stock; pp. 20–21, 21 (inset) by Maura B. McConnell; pp. 22–23 ©
Roger Allyn Lee/SuperStock.

Publisher Cataloging Data

Roza, Greg
  Heads or tails? : exploring probability through
games / Greg Roza.
        p. cm. — (PowerMath)
Includes index.
Summary: This book explores probability, the measure
of chance, in true-or-false questions, multiple-choice questions,
coin-tossing games, games using a spinner, and games played
with dice.
  ISBN 0-8239-8971-2 (hardcover)
  ISBN 0-8239-8894-5 (pbk)
  6-pack ISBN 0-8239-7422-7
  1. Probabilities—Juvenile literature
[1. Probabilities]   I. Title   II. Series
  2004
  519.2--dc21

Manufactured in the United States of America

Contents

What Is Probability?

Probability is the measure of the chance that an event will happen. We use probability every day when we describe events with words such as "likely," "unlikely," "certain," and "impossible." Will the Sun rise tomorrow? Certainly. Will I read a book tomorrow? It's likely. Will I see a shooting star tonight? It's unlikely. Will I grow wings and fly to the Moon? That's impossible!

certainly

likely

unlikely

If someone says "I like my chances," they are saying that they think the chance of something happening is good. If someone says "No chance," they are saying that they think an event could never happen.

True or False?

Probability is often written as a fraction. If you don't know the answer to a true-or-false question, you still have a 1-in-2 chance of getting it right. This means that out of 2 possible answers, 1 is correct. So the probability of choosing the correct answer is $\frac{1}{2}$, or 1 out of 2.

fraction

$\frac{1}{2}$ number of correct answers

number of possible answers

If you try to guess the answer to a true-or-false question, the chance of getting the question right and the chance of getting it wrong are equal. However, if you don't answer the question at all, you have no chance of getting it right.

What if you don't know the answer to a **multiple-choice question** with 4 possible answers? You have a 1-in-4 chance—or a $\frac{1}{4}$ chance—of choosing the correct answer.

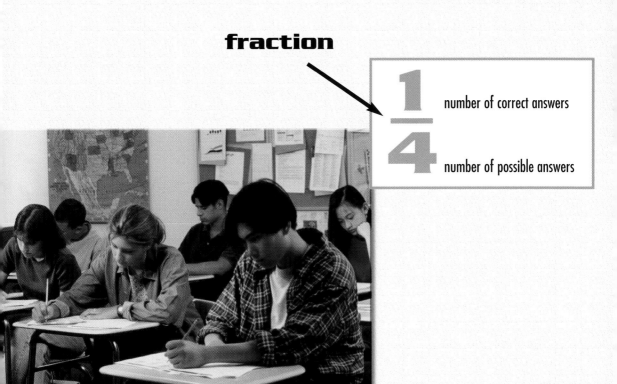

fraction

$\dfrac{1}{4}$ number of correct answers
number of possible answers

heads

tails

$$\frac{1}{2}$$ number of correct guesses

number of possible choices

Heads or Tails?

The probability of guessing the result of a coin toss is $\frac{1}{2}$, or 1 correct guess out of 2 possible choices. It is equally likely that the coin will land heads up or tails up. This is called an equal chance.

Before a football game, the **referee** tosses a coin and asks one team to call "heads" or "tails." This is a fair way to choose which team gets the ball first. Each team has an equal chance of winning the coin toss.

If the referee flipped the coin 100 times, probability says that the coin would land heads up 50 times, or $\frac{1}{2}$ of the time, and tails up 50 times, or $\frac{1}{2}$ of the time. It is not certain that heads and tails will each land face up 50 times, but it is more likely than either one landing face up 100 times.

Toss a Coin

You can play a coin-tossing game with a friend. Toss the coin and call "heads" or "tails" while it is in the air. After 10 tosses, how many times did the coin land heads up? How many times did the coin land tails up? Remember, it is not certain that the coin will land heads up half the time and tails up half the time. Record the results in a table like the one shown here. Also record how many times you were right and how many times your friend was right. The person who guessed correctly most often is the winner.

Round	1	2	3	4	5	6	7	8	9	10	
Result of Coin Toss	H	T	T	H	H	T	H	H	T	H	Total
Jan's Guess	H	H	T	T	H	T	H	T	T	H	7 out of 10
Nick's Guess	T	T	H	H	T	H	H	H	H	H	5 out of 10

T= tails
H= heads

☐ correct guess
☐ incorrect guess

According to this chart, Jan won the game of heads or tails. Out of 10 coin tosses, she correctly guessed the result 7 times. Nick correctly guessed the result 5 times. For 2 of the tosses, both Nick and Jan correctly guessed "heads."

Let's Take a Spin

Some games use a spinner. This spinner has 2 colors, green and blue. Each color is $\frac{1}{2}$ of the whole spinner. Chances are that the arrow will land on green $\frac{1}{2}$ of the time and blue $\frac{1}{2}$ of the time.

Let's say someone asks you to guess how many times the arrow will land on green out of 10 spins. Probability says that it will land on green $\frac{1}{2}$ of the time, so a good guess would be 5 times. This is called making an **estimate**.

We make an estimate when we need a quick answer without taking time to figure out the exact answer. An estimate is a guess you make using facts you already know and math skills you have already learned.

5 out of 10 spins = $\frac{1}{2}$ of the spins

Put a Spin on It

Not all spinners look the same. This spinner has 4 equal **sections**, 2 green and 2 blue. Chances are the arrow will still land on green $\frac{1}{2}$ of the time because $\frac{1}{2}$ of the spinner is still green.

$\frac{1}{3}$ 1 spin
3 possible outcomes

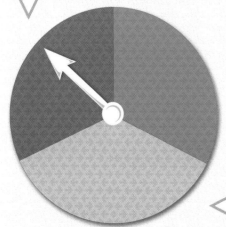

$\frac{1}{2}$ 1 spin
2 possible outcomes

This spinner has 3 colors. What is the probability that the arrow will land on green? Green is 1 result out of 3 possible results, so the probability is 1 out of 3, or $\frac{1}{3}$.

This spinner has 4 equal sections that are all different colors. Each color is $\frac{1}{4}$ of the whole spinner. You can estimate that the arrow will land on green 1 out of 4 times, or $\frac{1}{4}$ of the time.

$\frac{1}{4}$ 1 spin
4 possible outcomes

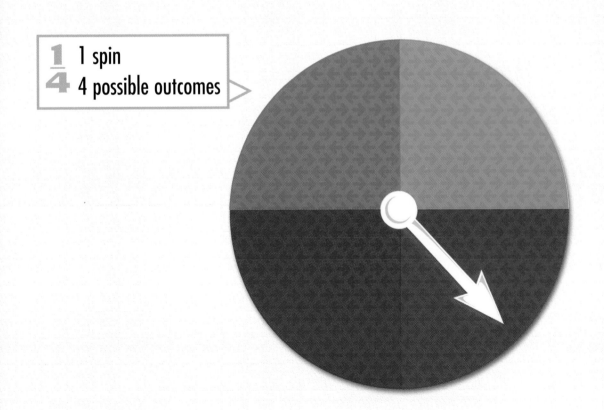

Roll Your Dice

Some games are played with **dice**. A die is $\frac{1}{2}$ of a pair of dice. A die has 6 sides, which are marked with 1 to 6 dots. When a die is thrown, there is a 1-in-6 chance of any number landing face up. Another way to say this is chances are that $\frac{1}{6}$ of your rolls will be a 1.

Let's say that you and a friend are playing a game with a die. Your friend rolls a 3. What are the chances that you will roll a higher number?

$\frac{1}{6}$ of 6 rolls = 1 roll

There are three numbers higher than 3 on a 6-sided die: 4, 5, and 6. That means that you have 3 out of 6 chances to beat the 3 your friend rolled.

Dice Chart

Possible Combinations

| 2 |
| 3 |
| 4 |
| 5 |
| 6 |
| 7 |
| 8 |
| 9 |
| 10 |
| 11 |
| 12 |

UH OH!
LOSE 100 POINTS!

When rolling 2 dice, the numbers on both dice are added together. It is possible to roll any number from 2 to 12 with 2 dice. Some numbers, however, are more likely to turn up than others. The most likely result is a 7 because there are 6 possible ways to roll that number. The least likely results are 2 and 12 because there is only 1 possible **combination** for each of those numbers when rolling 2 dice. This chart shows that there are a total of 36 possible combinations when rolling 2 dice.

Some board games use 2 dice. Which space on a board game do you think is landed on the most when the game first begins? The seventh space is landed on most often, because 7 is the most likely outcome when rolling 2 dice.

Fun with Marbles

If you place 4 blue marbles and 1 green marble in a bag, what are the chances that you will pick the green marble on the first try? There is 1 chance to get a green marble out of 5 possible results. This can be shown by using the fraction $\frac{1}{5}$.

Let's say the first marble chosen was blue. That leaves 3 blue marbles and 1 green marble. Now there are 4 possible results, but there is still 1 chance to get a green marble. So the chance of getting a green marble is 1 in 4, or $\frac{1}{4}$.

What are the chances of picking a blue marble on the first try? There are 4 out of 5 chances of picking a blue marble, or $\frac{4}{5}$. You are more likely to pick a blue marble than a green marble on the first try.

Winning Probability

You can use the bag of marbles to play a game. Put 8 marbles in a bag—7 blue ones and 1 green one. Who will pick the green marble first? There are 8 marbles to choose from, so the first person has a 1 out of 8, or $\frac{1}{8}$, chance of picking the green marble. Let's say the first person picks a blue marble. What is the probability that the second person will pick a green marble? Now there are 7 marbles to choose from, but still only 1 green marble, so the probability is 1 out of 7, or $\frac{1}{7}$. The fewer marbles there are in the bag, the better your chances are of picking the green marble!

Glossary

combination (kahm-buh-NAY-shun) A single thing made by joining or mixing two or more different things.

dice (DISE) A pair of small blocks marked on each side with 1 to 6 dots. Dice are used in many games.

estimate (ESS-tuh-muht) A careful guess about amount, size, or value.

multiple-choice question (MUHL-tuh-puhl–CHOIS KWES-chun) A question on a test with 3 or more possible answers, from which a student must choose the 1 right answer.

probability (prah-buh-BIH-luh-tee) A measure of the chance that an event will happen.

referee (reh-fuh-REE) A person who makes sure players follow the rules during a game or sports event.

section (SEK-shun) A part of something larger.

Index